HEINZ

ESTP 1869 ESTP

CELEBRATING
THE BEST OF BRITISH

50 Easy Heinz recipes from Top Celebrities and Chefs

Edited by Becky Johnson

SIMON & SCHUSTER
A VIACOM COMPANY

First published in Great Britain by Simon & Schuster UK Ltd, 2002
A Viacom Company

Copyright © 2002 H J Heinz Company Ltd

Simon & Schuster UK Ltd
Africa House
64–78 Kingsway
London
WC2B 6AH

1 3 5 7 9 10 8 6 4 2

Design: Jane Humphrey
Editorial and typesetting: Grapevine Publishing Services Ltd
Photography: Steve Lee
Home economist: Sian Davies
Stylist for food photography: Marian Price

Printed and bound in China

ISBN 0 74323 214 3

V denotes a vegetarian recipe and assumes that free-range eggs
and vegetarian cheese are used

CONTENTS

INTRODUCTION For generations now Heinz has been at the heart of British food. Whether it's the traditional breakfast, bangers and mash or fish and chips, they'd all be unimaginable to us Brits without the addition of one of Heinz's many varieties.

In the Golden Jubilee year this book takes Heinz's passion for simple, healthy and reliable food one step further and, using the nation's favourite foods, celebrates the best of British cooking. The book has been created to support the work of I CAN, the only charity dedicated to helping over one million British children with speech and language difficulties.

Fifty top British celebrities take the starring roles – their ideas and recipes that fill these pages. We've had a huge variety of recipes put forward, from simple new twists on old classics to inventive family favourites. The enthusiasm with which the recipes have been offered has not only made my job a pleasure, but also revealed the special role that Heinz plays in British lives.

Within this book you'll find five chapters of bright ideas to tempt the tastebuds. With such a wealth of snacks and meals to satisfy everyone from the peckish to the ravenous, we hope it will be the book that busy British cooks will reach for time and time again.

I CAN is the national educational charity for children with speech and language difficulties. Being able to communicate is something most of us take for granted whether we're talking to friends, listening to the radio, or reading stories to our children. For most of us, learning to communicate is something that happens naturally from the moment we are born.

But for one in ten children this just doesn't happen. Imagine being a child living in a world where everyone seems to speak a foreign language and words come out jumbled. And, because you can't communicate, no matter how hard you try, you are labelled as backwards or idle. This is what life can be like for the million children in the UK with speech and language difficulties. Unless they get the right help at the right time, these children struggle at school and may not even gain basic literacy and numeracy skills.

Through this recipe book, Heinz and I CAN have come together to raise awareness of the importance of mealtimes, not only as a time to enjoy the healthy and fun food of Heinz, but also as an opportunity to help develop young children's speech and language skills. Mealtime eating is a sociable activity – the earliest opportunities for children to communicate often revolve around eating, demanding and refusing food as babies. Eating and drinking involve many of the same muscles involved in speaking and help develop a young child's awareness and control of their lips and tongue.

What's more, this excellent collection of recipes is. about celebrating British heritage. As I CAN is one of the charities officially nominated to benefit on the occasion of the Golden Jubilee, it's only fitting that we help salute the great British mealtime.

Thank you for buying this book. By doing so, you have made an important contribution to I CAN's work.

Gill Edelman, Chief Executive of I CAN

CELEBRATING THE HISTORY OF HEINZ Over the last century, Heinz products have come to occupy a prime place on our supermarket shelves and kitchen table. Indeed, such is the place of Heinz products at the heart of British home cooking that it's hard to imagine British life without them.

Henry J Heinz made his first trip to Europe in 1886, bringing with him samples of his products. His first stop was at Fortnum & Mason, London's most prestigious grocery store. On tasting the samples, Fortnum's head of purchasing famously declared "I think, Mr Heinz, we will take the lot." From this promising start, it wasn't long before Heinz became well known for its product quality and reliability. In 1905, Heinz bought its first factory in Britain, marking the beginning of the well-loved tradition of Heinz in the UK.

In 1928 the first can of Heinz Baked Beans was produced at the Kitt Green factory in Wigan, with Heinz Spaghetti following two years later. Since then, Heinz products have become one of the most loved staples of British life. In fact, one of the best loved Heinz products, Heinz Salad Cream, is a uniquely British invention, used to liven up the often dull and unimaginative foods available during years of rationing after the war.

Heinz advertising has also been a vital part of British life, from the days in the late 1800s when huge signs were seen beside railway lines to the first TV commercials in the late 1950s. "Beanz Meanz Heinz" is one of the company's most enduring slogans — first used in the 1960s, the catchphrase ran for 22 years. It still remains part of the British consciousness today, with industry experts recently voting it the best advertising slogan of all time.

Heinz has also broken new ground with its competitions. Most famous of all is the 1961 soup competition, in which 57 Minis were offered as prizes and all entrants received a

To celebrate the Golden Jubilee
Heinz has recreated one of Britain's
best-loved landmarks in its own iconic style.
For many Tower Bridge is one of the most
enduring symbols of the British landscape.
As a celebration of the Best of British Heinz
have decided to construct the bridge using
its own products, shown on the right.

Heinz's tribute to a fellow British
institution can be easily made in any
kitchen. Simply use sausages and
cocktail sticks to build the bridge.
Then toast the bread to make the banks
and use Heinz baked beans to create
the River Thames.

can of soup. The competition attracted huge amounts of publicity and was heralded as "the biggest promotion that ever hit the grocery trade".

Today, Britain's love affair with Heinz remains as strong as ever. Indeed, the facts speak for themselves, with over 1.2 million cans of Heinz Baked Beans eaten every day in the UK. As a healthy and easy meal choice, Heinz products simply can't be beaten. The recipes in this book demonstrate both the versatility and enduring appeal of the products, which we hope will continue to nourish and satisfy "the Best of British" for many years to come.

BREAKFASTZ AND BRUNCHEZ

A traditional breakfast is a great British institution. This chapter brings new ideas to the first meal of the day, with suggestions for light to hearty breakfasts and lazy brunches.

CHAPTER
1

KATE MOSS At last! The secret of what Britain's most famous supermodel eats every morning is out! This recipe for Boston Baked Beans is a quick and easy twist on Beans on Toast and tastes great served on hot, buttered muffins. Definitely worth getting out of bed for!

BOSTON BAKED BEANS

1   Remove the rind from the bacon and slice it into 1 cm (½ inch) wide lardons. Fry the bacon in its own fat in a large frying pan or casserole until golden and just crispy. Add the onion and garlic and cook a further 5 minutes, until softened.

2   Add all the other ingredients except the parsley, and stir. Cover and cook for 10 minutes then serve on hot, buttered muffins. Sprinkle parsley on top.

 Serves 4

Preparation 5 minutes
Cooking 10 minutes

8 rashers bacon
2 onions, finely chopped
1 clove garlic, crushed
1 tbsp mustard powder
2 tbsp brown sugar
4 tbsp golden syrup
2 x 415 g can Heinz Baked Beans
2 tbsp Worcestershire Sauce
2 tbsp Heinz Tomato Ketchup
small bunch fresh parsley, chopped, to garnish

SARA COX This favourite Radio One breakfast DJ has early morning wake-up calls that put the rest of us to shame. On those mornings when Sara needs a bit of extra fuel to get her going, this hearty breakfast is the answer. It's a new and easy version of the classic Scottish dish — and tastes fantastic.

SMOKED HADDOCK KEDGEREE

1   Cook the rice with the saffron in plenty of boiling water for 10–15 minutes, or until tender. Drain the rice, pouring the boiling water over the haddock. Leave to stand for 5 minutes.

2   Drain the fish and remove the skin and any bones then flake coarsely and set aside.

3   Heat the oil in a large frying pan or wok then add the onion and fry for 5 minutes, until softened. Add the curry powder and all the other ingredients including the cooked fish and rice.

4   Fold gently together and heat through for 5 minutes then serve.

Serves 4

Preparation + cooking 40 minutes

175 g (6 oz) easy-cook long-grain rice

a pinch of saffron threads (optional)

225 g (8 oz) smoked haddock

1 tbsp vegetable oil

1 medium-sized onion, finely chopped

1 tbsp curry powder
    (or 1 tsp each ground coriander, cumin,
    fennel, turmeric, black mustard seed)

400 g (14 oz) can Heinz Spring Vegetable Soup

2 medium eggs, hard boiled, sliced into quarters

small bunch fresh parsley, chopped

150 ml (¼ pint) crème fraîche or plain yogurt

JANE ASHER "Cooking and enjoying a meal with others is one of life's simple pleasures. But for many children, speech and language difficulties impair their ability to socialise and can make such occasions difficult, if not frightening. I CAN works to help children overcome these problems and I am delighted to be supporting their excellent work."

SALMON FISHCAKES

1   Remove any bones from the fish, then mix with the potato, parsley or chives, Salad Cream and seasoning.
2   Divide the mixture into 8 and shape each piece into a 1 cm (½ inch) thick round.
3   Roll each fishcake in the flour, then dip into the beaten egg and finally cover in breadcrumbs. Chill for 20 minutes to firm up a little.
4   Heat the oil in a frying pan and fry the fishcakes gently, in batches as necessary, for about 2–3 minutes on each side, until golden brown and cooked through.

 Serves 4
Preparation + cooking 30 minutes
+ 20 minutes chilling time
300 g (10½ oz) fresh, cooked or canned salmon, drained and flaked
300 g (10½ oz) potatoes, peeled, boiled and mashed
small bunch fresh parsley or chives, chopped
4 tbsp Heinz Salad Cream
2 tbsp plain flour, seasoned
1 medium egg, beaten
75 g (2¾ oz) fresh breadcrumbs
2 tbsp vegetable or peanut oil
salt and freshly ground black pepper

LOUIS EMERICK Avid viewers of Brookside will know Louis Emerick as Mick Johnson. Mick worked for a while in a chip shop and a portion of chips would be an ideal accompaniment to this omelette. Or simply serve on its own for a lighter start to the day.

CHEESE & HERB OMELETTE

1   Melt the butter in a small frying pan or omelette pan and meanwhile beat all the ingredients except the cheese together in a bowl.
2   Pour the omelette mixture into the pan and cook over a low heat until it starts to set. Sprinkle the grated cheese on top and cook until fully melted. Flip the omelette in half and tip out of the pan onto a plate to serve.

 V Serves 1
Preparation 5 minutes
Cooking 6 minutes
1 tbsp butter
1 tbsp Heinz Salad Cream
2 eggs
2 tbsp milk
small bunch fresh chives, parsley, coriander, tarragon, mint or basil, chopped
50 g (1¾ oz) Cheddar cheese, grated
salt and freshly ground black pepper

LIGHT MEALZ AND LUNCHEZ

'Beanz Meanz Heinz' first entered into the popular consciousness in the 1960s and since then we've discovered people love to eat all kinds of things with their Heinz Baked Beans. This chapter starts with five celebrities revealing their secret when it comes to the Perfect Beans on Toast. It's also the place to look for simple twists to make dishes more exciting, such as Perfect Potato Salad and Quick and Eazy Samosas.

CHAPTER

2

JEREMY CLARKSON Everyone seems to have their own ideas on how to make the Perfect Beans on Toast. TV presenter Jeremy certainly doesn't claim to be hot stuff in the kitchen, but he is very certain on how he likes his beans. "I only have one recipe – this is it. You must use Heinz Baked Beans – no imitations are allowed."

PERFECT BEANS ON TOAST NO. 1

1   Find a can opener, open can of beans. Put beans in saucepan with two large knobs of butter and the Tabasco.

2   Heat the beans slowly over a low heat for a long time, until the mixture becomes slightly mushy. The beans must still resemble the shape of a bean but the mixture must be mushy.

3   Place two slices of bread in the toaster and toast lightly. Butter the toast liberally, making sure that the butter reaches every corner.

4   Place the beans all over the toast and serve immediately.

V Serves 1
Preparation 2 minutes
Cooking 5 minutes

200 g (7 oz) can Heinz Baked Beans
lashings of butter
6 drops Tabasco
good white bread

PHIL VICKERY Celebrity chef Phil Vickery likes to add a bit of kick to his Baked Beans. His version certainly packs a punch — with chilli, fresh coriander and honey as the perfect additions. Why not try it yourself and see?

PERFECT BEANS ON TOAST NO. 2

1 Toast the bread then butter while hot. Meanwhile, heat through the Baked Beans.
2 Stir in the chilli, honey and coriander and spoon onto the toast. Serve immediately.

 **Serves 1**
Preparation 5 minutes
Cooking 3 minutes
2 thick slices crusty white bread
butter to spread on toast
200 g (7 oz) can Heinz Baked Beans
1 small red chilli, deseeded and finely chopped
1 tsp runny honey
handful fresh coriander, chopped

NATALIE APPLETON Beans have never, ever tasted so good! For pop star Natalie, the perfect addition is some good English cheese. It's a quick and healthy meal for people with frantic lives — just like Natalie, who says she loves this recipe as it's "quick and easy — great, as I am always on the go!"

PERFECT BEANS ON TOAST NO. 3

1 Mix the cheese with the seasonings and milk in a bowl. Heat the grill and toast the bread — one side should only be toasted lightly. Meanwhile heat the baked beans.
2 Spread the cheese mixture onto the less toasted side of the bread and grill until bubbling and golden. Pour over the hot beans and eat.

 Serves 1
Preparation 2 minutes
Cooking 5 minutes
100 g (3½ oz) mature Cheddar cheese, grated
1 tsp dry mustard powder
freshly ground black pepper
1 tsp Worcestershire sauce
2 tbsp milk
2 thick slices granary bread
200 g (7 oz) can Heinz Baked Beans

LAURENCE LLEWELYN-BOWEN Flamboyant interior designer Laurence admits he is not always at home in the kitchen. "I may be known for my exotic room designs, but my family are not used to seeing me use such flair when it comes to cooking. My own personal variation on Beans on Toast, however, is not only pleasing on the eye, but also meets with the tastes of the more sophisticated palates."

PERFECT BEANS ON TOAST NO. 4

1   Slice the ciabatta in half lengthways and toast it. Heat the grill and place the toasted ciabatta slices on the grill pan. Heat through the Baked Beans.
2   Spoon the beans on top of the toast. Scatter over the cheese and black pepper then grill until bubbling.

⊞ Ⓥ Serves 1
Preparation 2 minutes
Cooking 5 minutes
½ ciabatta loaf
200 g (7 oz) can Heinz Baked Beans
50 g (1¾ oz) Dolcelatte cheese
    or Bleu d'Auvergne, crumbled
freshly ground black pepper

ROWAN ATKINSON Who else to ask about Perfect Beans on Toast than Mr. Bean himself? It's our tongue in cheek recipe ... it's so simple, the only thing that's complicated about it is remembering not to burn the toast!

PERFECT BEANS ON TOAST NO. 5

1   Heat the beans in a pan until they go all bubbly.
2   Pour over toast and serve.

⊞ Ⓥ Serves 1
Preparation 2 minutes
Cooking 5 minutes

200 g (7 oz) can Heinz Baked Beans
2 slices buttered toast

BEN FREEMAN Fans of Emmerdale will recognise actor Ben Freeman as the soap's heart-throb, Scott. During a long, hard day on the Emmerdale set, these Samosas are the perfect choice — quick and easy to prepare, they are a great snack to fill the gap until dinnertime. A delicious alternative to sandwiches — try them for a packed lunch or in a picnic.

QUICK AND EAZY SAMOSAS

1   Preheat the oven to Gas Mark 7/220°C/425°F. Blend one can of the Heinz Curried Beans, chickpeas and coriander to a rough paste in a food processor then stir in the other can.

2   Lay one sheet of filo on a work surface and cut it into 3 strips. Brush lightly with the oil then place a dessertspoonful of the bean mixture at one end of the strip.

3   Turn one corner diagonally over the filling to meet the long edge of the strip. Continue folding the pastry, keeping the triangular shape as you work.

4   Transfer to a baking sheet and brush with more oil. Repeat with the other samosas then bake for 10–15 minutes until golden and crisp.

V Makes about 18
Preparation 20 minutes
Cooking 10–15 minutes
2 x 200 g (7 oz) cans Heinz Curried Beans
400 g (14 oz) chickpeas, drained
small bunch fresh coriander
4 sheets filo pastry, defrosted
4 tbsp or more of vegetable oil or melted butter

SIR HENRY COOPER, OBE KSG "This recipe packs a punch and is great after a hard day at work as winter nights draw in," says boxing veteran Sir Henry. His version of mash is a simple way to make potatoes that bit more special — serve with the best bangers you can get your hands on.

EXTRA CREAMY CHAMP

1   Cook the potatoes in boiling, salted water for 20–25 minutes until tender, then drain.
2   Meanwhile heat the milk in a small pan with the chopped spring onions. Mash the potatoes and beat in the spring onions, butter, Salad Cream and seasoning.

 V Serves 4

Preparation 10 minutes
Cooking 35 minutes
750 g (1 lb 10 oz) floury potatoes, peeled
   and cut into even-sized chunks
100 ml (3½ fl oz) milk
a bunch of spring onions, chopped
50 g (1¾ oz) butter
4 tbsp Heinz Salad Cream
salt and freshly ground black pepper

STEPHEN ARNOLD   Stephen Arnold is better known as Coronation Street's resident butcher, Ashley Peacock. This mash would taste a treat with some of Ashley's bangers — great for bringing a bit of the Mediterranean to Weatherfield.

TANGY MEDITERRANEAN MASH

1   Cook the potatoes in boiling, salted water for 20–25 minutes until tender, then drain.
2   Mash the potatoes and add the butter, Sundried Tomato Sauce and seasoning and beat together well, then serve, scattered with basil.

V Serves 4

Preparation 10 minutes
Cooking 35 minutes
750 g (1 lb 10 oz) floury potatoes,
   cut into even-sized chunks
50 g (1¾ oz) butter
6 tbsps Heinz Sundried Tomato Sauce
salt and freshly ground black pepper
fresh basil (optional), to garnish

JAMES REDMAN If you like hot 'n' spicy like TV presenter James, you'll love this one. The chillis give the crostini that little something extra. This makes a lovely lunch or a really special starter — ideal if you're trying to impress someone.

CHILLI BEAN AND CORIANDER CROSTINI

1 Drain most of the sauce from the beans. Finely chop one of the chillis and slice the other into thin slivers.

2 Purée all the ingredients except the bread and chilli slivers together in a food processor.

3 Spread the mixture on the toast slices and serve garnished with little sprigs of coriander and the slivers of red chilli.

V Serves 4

Preparation 5 minutes

415 g can Heinz Baked Beans

2 small red chillis, deseeded

1 tsp ground cumin

small bunch fresh coriander, chopped
   (reserve a few sprigs for garnish)

2 tbsp plain yogurt

1 French stick, sliced thinly on the diagonal
   and toasted, or use crispbreads

DOMINIC BRUNT This is a great recipe for the Emmerdale actor who plays Paddy in the long-running soap – a brilliant warming dish for a cold winter's day. Serve with some warm, crusty bread and you're sure to be a hit in the kitchen.

SOOTHING BEAN AND ROSEMARY SOUP

1   Heat the oil in a large saucepan then fry the onion, garlic and carrot for 5 minutes, until just beginning to soften.

2   Add all the other ingredients and bring to the boil. Liquidise the soup in a blender then return to the pan and heat through. Serve with a swirl of crème fraîche or Greek yogurt.

 Serves 4

Preparation 5 minutes

Cooking 15 minutes

1 tbsp olive oil

1 large onion, diced

2 garlic cloves, crushed

2 large carrots, diced

2 x 415 g can Heinz Baked Beans

4 sprigs rosemary, leaves removed from stem and finely chopped

1 litre (1¾ pints) vegetable stock

salt and freshly ground black pepper

crème fraîche or Greek yogurt, to serve

LAURA BAILEY An old favourite has been given a stylish makeover by model and beauty columnist Laura Bailey. This recipe is a great twist on Cream of Tomato soup – and an easy way of making a simple lunch that little bit extra-special.

CREAM OF TOMATO FLORENTINE SOUP

Heat through the soup and meanwhile place all the pesto ingredients in a food processor and blend to a paste. Serve the soup with a dollop of pesto on the top.

 Serves 2

Preparation 10 minutes

Cooking 5 minutes

400 g (14 oz) can Heinz Cream of Tomato Soup

For the Pesto

1 large bunch fresh basil or parsley or rocket (at least 50g / 1¾ oz)

1 large clove garlic, chopped

50 g (1¾ oz) Parmesan, freshly grated

50 g (1¾ oz) pine kernels, toasted

150 ml (¼ pint) olive oil

LIGHT MEALZ
AND
LUNCHEZ

CLARISSA DICKSON-WRIGHT According to celebrity chef and food-lover Clarissa, "Heinz Baked Beans are a wonderful comfort food and, if such things interest you, the only healthy fast food. I like to make this recipe as it reminds me of Spain. The eggs taste delicious and quite different. It makes an excellent supper dish or even a starter if done in individual pots."

SPANISH EGG AND BEAN SUPPER

1   Empty the can of beans into a small, flat saucepan or frying pan and stir in the chorizo strips. Make two wells in the top and crack in the eggs, making sure that they don't break.

2   Season and cook gently over a low flame until the beans are heated through and the eggs are cooked. Serve with fresh bread.

Serves 2
Preparation 5 minutes
Cooking 10 minutes
415 g can Heinz Baked Beans
75 g (2¾ oz) chorizo sausage, cut into strips
2 large eggs
salt and freshly ground black pepper
fresh bread, to serve

RICHARD WILSON This salad recipe is so quick and easy to throw together – simply mix together the ingredients and serve on brown toast. As an alternative salad, actor Richard Wilson recommends simply serving cold Baked Beans on their own. "I am a great fan of the cold Baked Bean Salad, cold meaning straight out of the fridge."

SMOKED MACKEREL AND HORSERADISH SALAD

1   Mix together the mackerel, celery and spring onions in a bowl.
2   Stir in the Salad Cream, horseradish and parsley and season with black pepper then serve with brown toast.

 Serves 4

Preparation 5–10 minutes

225 g (8 oz) smoked mackerel, skinned and flaked
2 sticks celery, finely chopped
4 spring onions, finely chopped
4 tbsp Heinz Salad Cream
1 tbsp creamed horseradish sauce
freshly ground black pepper
brown toast, to serve

ANNA BRECON As we know, Lady Tara has the highest standards, so only Perfect Potato Salad will do for this former actress from Emmerdale. Ideal for lazy summer days, this recipe is a great addition to any barbeque or picnic.

PERFECT POTATO SALAD

1   Cook the potatoes in boiling, salted water for about 25 minutes, until soft, then drain and return to the heat to dry out. Meanwhile grill the bacon until it is very crispy and crumble or cut it into pieces.

2   Combine the bacon and potatoes with all the other ingredients in a large bowl. In a small bowl stir the dressing ingredients together then pour over the salad and toss together while still warm.

Serves 6
Preparation 10 minutes
Cooking 25 minutes

**500 g (1 lb 2 oz) floury potatoes,
    cut into 2.5 cm (1 inch) cubes
6 rashers streaky bacon
2 hard-boiled eggs, chopped
1 large gherkin, finely chopped
small bunch chives, finely chopped
salt and freshly ground black pepper**
For the dressing
**4 tbsp Heinz Salad Cream
4 tbsp crème fraîche
small bunch fresh dill, chopped (optional)**

KIDZ MEALZ

Countless children have grown up on Heinz – these recipes take ingredients that kids love and serve them up in new, exciting and healthy ways. For children – and children at heart – they include some great speedy solutions, such as Saucy Potato Skins and Bright Bean Salad.

CHAPTER

3

SADIE FROST/JUDE LAW A great recipe from one of Britain's most famous celebrity couples. "This is an easy dish to make, tasty but still very nutritious, especially for veggies, and the kids love it. Sometimes we add some tofu for extra protein."

VEGGIE BEAN MOUSSAKA

1   Preheat the oven to Gas Mark 5/190°C/375°F. In a large frying pan fry the onion in 2 tbsp of the oil for 5 minutes, until softened, then add the garlic, peppers, courgettes, sweetcorn, dried herbs and seasoning. Cover and cook for 10 minutes.

2   Meanwhile heat the grill to high. Lay all the aubergine slices out in one layer on the grill pan (you may have to do them in two batches). Brush with 2 tbsp of the olive oil and season. Grill for 4 minutes, until browned.

3   Spoon half of the vegetable mixture into a deep ovenproof dish and cover with the Baked Beans and a little crumbled cheese, then arrange half the grilled aubergine on top.

4   Add another layer of vegetables, a little more crumbled cheese and another layer of aubergine slices. In a bowl, beat together the sour cream and eggs with seasoning and spread over the top.

5   Sprinkle with the remaining cheese and bake for 40–45 minutes, until golden brown.

V Serves 4–6
Preparation 20 minutes
Cooking 1 hour

1 large onion, finely chopped
4 tbsp olive oil
1 large clove garlic, crushed
1 yellow pepper, deseeded and finely chopped
1 red pepper, deseeded and finely chopped
2 large courgettes, finely chopped
200 g (7 oz) sweetcorn
2 tsp dried oregano or majoram
415 g can Heinz Baked Beans
2 medium aubergines, thinly sliced
200 g (7 oz) feta cheese, crumbled
300 ml (½ pint) sour cream or yogurt
2 eggs
salt and freshly ground black pepper

FLOELLA BENJAMIN Former Playschool presenter Floella shares one of her favourite recipes. "Mealtimes are a great way to get kids and adults together and share our day's experiences while we eat. But not all children have the language abilities to enjoy that simple task. That's why I'm supporting I CAN's work to give all children the golden gift of speech."

CHICKEN AND BEAN TORTILLAS

1   Preheat the oven to Gas Mark 6/200°C/400°F and place the chicken on a baking tray. Drizzle over the lime juice, oil and seasoning, toss lightly, then bake, covered with a sheet of foil, for 20 minutes. Remove the foil and bake for a further 10 minutes.

2   While the chicken is baking, mash the BBQ Beans with a fork and heat the oil in a frying pan. Fry the garlic until golden then add the beans and fry for 10 minutes, turning frequently until they are starting to dry out. Add the coriander and mix well.

3   Warm the tortillas quickly in the oven and then spoon the refried beans onto a strip down the middle of each. Top with the chicken and spoonfuls of guacamole and sour cream, then roll up to eat.

Serves 4
Preparation 10 minutes
Cooking 30 minutes
4 skinless, boneless chicken breasts, sliced into thin strips
juice of 2 limes
2 tbsp olive oil
salt and freshly ground black pepper
For the refried beans
2 x 200 g (7 oz) can Heinz Barbecue Beans
1 tbsp olive oil
1 clove garlic, crushed
small bunch fresh coriander, chopped
To serve
8 large, soft tortillas
250 g (8 oz) guacamole
300 ml (½ pint) sour cream

MELANIE BLATT Kids love helping out in the kitchen and this dish from pop star and mother Melanie is simple enough to let them work with you to put it together.

KIDZ PIZZA WITH BAKED BEANS

1   Preheat the oven to Gas Mark 6/200°C/400°F and spread the pizza base with the Baked Beans and Sausages.
2   Sprinkle over the herbs, if liked, and the cheese and bake for 10–15 minutes, until the edges are golden and the cheese bubbling.

Serves 2
Preparation 5 minutes
Cooking 10 minutes
18 cm (7 in) round ready-made pizza base
200 g (7 oz) can Heinz Baked Beans and
   Sausages
1 tsp dried oregano (optional)
100 g (3½ oz) Cheddar or Mozzarella cheese,
   grated

EMMA BUNTON Pop star Emma likes her Beanburgers as spicy as her music. Kids will also go mad for these vegetarian burgers. Serve with all the trimmings – lettuce, tomato, gherkins and lots and lots of Ketchup!

SPICY BEANBURGERS IN BAPS

1   Mix the mince with the garlic, parsley, mustard, Worcestershire sauce, chilli powder and ground cumin. Mash the Baked Beans into a mush with a fork then add them to the mince mixture and season. Shape into 4 thick burgers.
2   Dust each burger with flour and heat the oil in a large frying pan. Fry the burgers for 5–10 minutes on each side, until golden brown and cooked through.
3   Serve the burgers on the baps or bagels with lettuce, tomato, gherkins and Ketchup.

 Serves 4
Preparation 10 minutes
Cooking 10 minutes
400 g (14 oz) Quorn or other vegetarian mince
1 clove garlic, crushed
small bunch fresh parsley, chopped
1 tsp French mustard
2 tsp Worcestershire Sauce
½ tsp chilli powder
1 tsp ground cumin
415 g can Heinz Baked Beans
2 tbsp seasoned flour for dusting
2 tbsp olive oil
salt and freshly ground black pepper
To serve
4 baps or bagels, cut in half and toasted
lettuce leaves and sliced tomatoes
sliced gherkins
Heinz Tomato Ketchup

KIDZ
MEALZ

Spicy Beanburgers in Baps.

CLAIRE KING Potatoes are often viewed as basic but this dish from 'Bad Girls' actress Claire King will really make them stand out. Try it – we guarantee it will become a favourite with kids and adults alike.

SAUCY POTATO SKINS

1   Spoon the middle out of the potato skins and mash in a bowl. Place the skins on a baking tray and preheat the grill to medium.
2   Divide the mashed potato into 2 separate bowls. To one of the bowls, add the Gruyere, bacon and 2 tbsp of the Salad Cream and fold together.
3   To the other bowl of mashed potato, add the chicken, avocado and remaining Salad Cream and fold together. Spoon one of the mixtures into some of the potato skins and the other into the remaining potato skins. Grill for 2–4 minutes, until golden brown, then serve.

 Serves 4
Preparation 10 minutes
Cooking 5 minutes
8 small baked potatoes, sliced in half
   lengthways
4 tbsp Heinz Salad Cream
50 g (1¾ oz) Gruyere cheese, grated
4 rashers of bacon, grilled until crispy then
   chopped
1 cooked, skinless, boneless breast of chicken,
   chopped
1 avocado, peeled, stone removed and chopped

PATSY PALMER A great recipe for busy mums who are always on the go like actress Patsy Palmer. It's also an easy recipe to get kids involved in the kitchen – they simply have to throw all the ingredients together and mix. Child's play!

BRIGHT BEAN SALAD

Place all the ingredients together in a large bowl and toss to mix well. Spoon onto serving plates and eat with lots of crusty bread to mop up all the delicious juices.

Serves 4
Preparation 10 minutes
2 x 415 g cans Heinz Baked Beans
100 g (3½ oz) black olives, pitted and chopped
2 tbsp Heinz Sundried Tomato Sauce
200 g (7 oz) cherry tomatoes, chopped in half
small bunch fresh parsley, chopped
small bunch fresh basil, chopped
crusty bread, to serve

QUICK AND EAZY DINNERZ

Comfort food is at the heart of Heinz and this chapter helps you with new ideas to put meals together in a flash. It includes simple dishes like the Macaroni Cheese Soufflé and Chicken and Asparagus Pie. For those who want to be more adventurous the dinner ideas also include tantalising recipes for Thai Red Curry and Chinatown Sweet and Sour Pork.

CHAPTER

4

RICHARD BRIERS This is one of actor Richards Briers' favourite recipes. "During the Second World War, my mother-in-law used to make a weekly Shepherds' Pie for her husband and his colleagues in the fire service. Meat was rationed so she increased the amount of vegetables and always added Baked Beans. My wife cooked this for us when we were out of work actors and it became such a favourite that we still cook and eat it today."

SHEPHERDS' PIE

1   Preheat the oven to Gas Mark 6/200°C/400°F. Heat the oil in a large casserole and gently fry the garlic, onion, celery and pepper for 10 minutes, until softened.

2   Add the mince and turn and break up with a wooden spoon until browned all over. Season and add the remaining vegetables, tomatoes, Tomato Ketchup, Baked Beans, Worcestershire Sauce and stock and stir together.

3   Cover the casserole and place in the oven for 20 minutes while you cook the potatoes.

4   Mash the cooked potatoes with the milk, most of the butter and seasoning. Remove the mince mixture from the oven and stir in the chopped herbs then cover with the mash. Make patterns on the top with a fork and dot with the remaining butter.

5   Return to the oven for 30 minutes, until the top is browned well, then serve.

Serves 4
Preparation 30 minutes
Cooking 1 hour

2 tsp olive oil
2 garlic cloves, crushed
1 medium onion, finely chopped
2 sticks celery, chopped
1 red pepper, cored, de-seeded and finely chopped
500 g (1 lb 2 oz) minced beef or lamb
4 medium carrots, finely diced
200 g (7 oz) mushrooms, chopped or a small can of sweetcorn, drained
400 g (14 oz) can Heinz Chopped Tomatoes
1½ tbsp Heinz Tomato Ketchup
415 g can Heinz Baked Beans
dash of Worcestershire sauce
300 ml (½ pint) stock
1 kg (2 lb 4 oz) potatoes, cut into chunks
5-6 tbsp milk
50 g (1¾ oz) butter
small bunch fresh herbs – e.g. parsley, tarragon, basil, chives – chopped
salt and freshly ground black pepper

MEG MATTHEWS "There is nothing more enjoyable on a winter's evening than Sizzling Sausages with my daughter Anais," says celebrity mother Meg. Sizzling Sausages never tasted as great as in this simple yet satisfying hotpot.

SIZZLING SAUSAGE AND BBQ BEAN POT

1   Heat the oil in a large frying pan or casserole and brown the sausage pieces. Remove the sausages with a slotted spoon and fry the onions, garlic and peppers in the left-over oil.

2   Add the chilli and replace the sausages in the pan, then add the beans and any seasoning required. Cover and cook for 10 minutes.

3   Stir in the fresh parsley or coriander and serve with crusty bread and potato wedges.

 Serves 4–6
Preparation 5 minutes
Cooking 15 minutes

8 sausages, cut into bite-sized pieces
1 tbsp olive oil
1 large onion, thinly sliced
1 clove garlic, crushed
2 red peppers, deseeded and finely diced
1 small red chilli, deseeded and finely chopped
4 x 200 g (7 oz) can Heinz Barbecue Beans
small bunch parsley or coriander, chopped
salt and freshly ground black pepper
crusty bread and potato wedges, to serve

BRIGIT FORSYTH Actress Brigit Forsyth has certainly risen to the occasion with this ideal recipe for entertaining the "likely lads". We challenge you to find an easier or tastier recipe for soufflé than this – a great way to impress in the kitchen!

MACARONI CHEESE SOUFFLÉ

1   Preheat the oven to Gas Mark 4/180°C/350°F. Grease the inside of a soufflé dish with the olive oil. Sprinkle with the Parmesan so that the inside of the dish is covered.

2   In a bowl mix the egg yolks with the Macaroni Cheese and lightly season if necessary.

3   In a clean bowl whisk the egg whites until they hold stiff peaks then fold into the macaroni mixture. Spoon into the soufflé dish and bake for 15–20 minutes until risen and golden. Serve immediately.

 V Serves 6

Preparation 5 minutes
Cooking 20 minutes

1 tbsp olive oil
100 g (3½ oz) Parmesan, finely grated
3 large eggs, separated
400 g (14 oz) can Heinz Macaroni Cheese
salt and freshly ground black pepper

CHRIS EUBANK What a knock-out recipe from boxer Chris! A really satisfying meal to make at the end of a long, hard day. Try it once and you'll be won over.

JAMBALAYA

1   Place the rice in a pan with 225 ml (8 fl oz) water and bring to the boil. Cover and simmer for 10 minutes, until the water has been absorbed.

2   Meanwhile, in a large frying pan, wok or casserole, fry the chicken, onion and garlic in the butter for 5 minutes. Add the rice, soup, cinnamon and cayenne pepper. Cover and simmer gently for 10 minutes, stirring occasionally.

3   Add the ham and parsley and stir through, then cook for a further 5 minutes until the rice is just tender. Check the seasoning and serve.

 Serves 4

Preparation 10 minutes
Cooking 30 minutes

225 g (8 oz) long-grain rice
225 g (8 oz) skinless, boneless chicken breast,
    diced
1 onion, peeled and chopped
1 clove garlic, crushed
25 g (1 oz) butter
400 g (14 oz) can Heinz Cream of Chicken Soup
1 tsp ground cinnamon
½ tsp cayenne pepper
350 g (12 oz) ham, diced
small bunch fresh parsley, chopped
salt and freshly ground black pepper

DONNA AIR This is a great vegetarian recipe for kids on the go and something TV presenter Donna loves cooking for herself. "You might not think it, but I'm a real traditional girl at heart — at my happiest in a warm country kitchen and cooking up a hearty meal."

SHEPHERDESS PIE

1   Preheat the oven to Gas Mark 6/200°C/400°F. Heat the oil in a large saucepan and gently fry the leek, courgette, carrot, garlic and mushrooms. Once warmed through, cover and cook, stirring frequently, for 10 minutes, or until the vegetables are soft.

2   Add the lentils, tomatoes, herbs and 425 ml (¾ pint) water. Bring the mixture to the boil, then reduce and simmer for 30 minutes or until the lentils are soft and the mixture thick. Meanwhile boil the potatoes for about 15 minutes, until soft.

3   Stir the Tomato Ketchup and Baked Beans into the lentil and vegetable mixture and cook for a further 5 minutes. Mash the potatoes, adding milk and seasoning.

4   Spoon the lentil mixture into a large, ovenproof dish. Spread the mashed potatoes over the top and bake in the oven for 15–20 minutes or until the potato is crispy.

 Serves 4

Preparation 10 minutes

Cooking 1 hour

2 tsp olive oil

1 leek, finely chopped

1 courgette, diced

1 carrot, diced

2 garlic cloves, crushed

125 g (4½ oz) mushrooms, sliced

125 g (4½ oz) dried, split red lentils

200 g (7 oz) can Heinz Chopped Tomatoes

1 tsp dried mixed herbs

1½ tbsp Heinz Tomato Ketchup

200 g (7 oz) can Heinz Baked Beans

1 kg (2 lb 4 oz) potatoes, cut into chunks

5-6 tbsp milk

salt and pepper

VIC REEVES A shooting star in the kitchen, this recipe from comic Vic always goes with a bang. A great way to create fireworks in the kitchen, this dish is ready and on the table in less time than it takes to order a Chinese take-away.

BANG BANG CHICKEN

1 Break the noodles into small pieces and soak them in very hot water for 5 minutes then drain (or cook as instructed on the packet). Blend the garlic and coriander (reserving a little for garnish) in a food processor until smooth.

2 Add the peanut butter, Ketchup, soy sauce, honey, chilli and lime or lemon and blend until it forms a smooth sauce, adding a little water if too thick.

3 Spread a pile of warm noodles onto the serving plates and top with the chicken and cucumber. Pour over the sauce, and scatter with the reserved coriander to serve.

Serves 4
Preparation 15 minutes
Cooking 5 minutes

125 g (4½ oz) Chinese glass noodles
6 cloves garlic, crushed
small bunch coriander, no roots, chopped
175 g (6 oz) smooth peanut butter
2 tbsp Heinz Tomato Ketchup
2 tbsp light soy sauce
2 tbsp runny honey
1 tsp chilli powder
juice of a lime or lemon
3 cooked skinless, boneless chicken breasts, shredded
1 cucumber, cut into fine strips

JACK DEE The flavour of this Mushroom Risotto from the comedian Jack Dee is as intense as the man himself. Serve with lots of grated Parmesan Cheese for a truly delicious supper.

INTENSE MUSHROOM RISOTTO

1   Place the dried mushrooms in a measuring jug and add 150 ml (¼ pint) boiling water. Heat the oil in a large, heavy saucepan and gently stir fry the onion and garlic until softened.

2   Add the rice and stir to mix well, then add the wine. Drain the dried mushrooms, reserving the water, and chop into small pieces. Strain the soaking water through a fine mesh sieve and add to the risotto with the chopped mushrooms.

3   Add the stock in small quantities, cooking and stirring frequently until all of it has been absorbed. Add the Mushroom Soup and continue to stir until the rice is tender and creamy.

4   Check the seasoning and stir in the parsley and most of the grated Parmesan before serving. Serve with the remaining Parmesan sprinkled over the top.

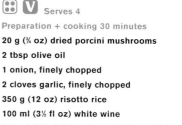 Serves 4

Preparation + cooking 30 minutes

20 g (¾ oz) dried porcini mushrooms
2 tbsp olive oil
1 onion, finely chopped
2 cloves garlic, finely chopped
350 g (12 oz) risotto rice
100 ml (3½ fl oz) white wine
850 ml (1½ pints) hot vegetable or chicken stock
400 g (14 oz) can Heinz Mushroom Soup
small bunch parsley, chopped
100 g (3½ oz) Parmesan cheese, grated
salt and freshly ground black pepper

JOHNNY VEGAS "Man cannot live on crisps alone — despite what monkey says."
Wise words indeed from the stand-up comic Johnny Vegas. As an alternative to crisps, try
this recipe for Thai Red Chicken Curry. See which you prefer!

THAI RED CHICKEN CURRY

1 Cut the pumpkin or squash into bite-sized pieces and parboil them.

2 Chop the chicken breasts into bite-sized pieces. Heat the oil in a large saucepan or wok and brown the chicken. Season and add the curry paste and spring onions. Stir fry for 2 minutes then add all the other ingredients except the coriander and peanuts.

3 Bring to a gentle simmer, stirring occasionally. Cook for 20 minutes, until the vegetables
are tender.

4 Serve scattered with the peanuts and fresh coriander.

Serves 4
Preparation 15 minutes
Cooking 25 minutes

450 g (1 lb) pumpkin or butternut squash
4 skinless, boneless chicken breasts
1 tbsp vegetable oil
2 tbsp Thai Red Curry Paste
1 bunch spring onions, sliced into 2.5 cm
   (1 inch) lengths
200 ml (7 fl oz) chicken or vegetable stock
400 g (14 oz) can Heinz Carrot and
   Coriander Soup
400 g (14 oz) can coconut milk
225 g (8 oz) potatoes, diced and par-boiled
150 g (5½ oz) bamboo shoots, drained and
   rinsed
2 tbsp fish sauce
2 tsp brown sugar
salt and freshly ground black pepper
small bunch fresh coriander, chopped, to serve
4 tbsp peanuts, toasted and chopped, to serve

CHRIS TARRANT Television presenter and DJ Chris says, "As a keen fisherman, the Roasted Cod Provencale is my perfect dinner choice." This dish is really quick to pull together, leaving you plenty of time to phone a friend!

COD PROVENÇALE

1   Preheat the oven to Gas Mark 5/190°C/375°F. In a large frying pan, fry the onion and garlic in the oil for 5 minutes, until softened.

2   Add the peppers, herbes de Provence and seasoning and stir fry for a further 10 minutes, until the peppers are softened and browned on the edges. Transfer to the bottom of an ovenproof dish, place the cod steaks on top and season again.

3   Pour the Heinz Cream of Tomato Soup over the top then scatter with the sundried tomatoes. Cover and bake for 35–40 minutes.

4   Scatter with the fresh basil to serve.

 Serves 4

Preparation 10 minutes

Cooking 50–55 minutes

1 large onion, sliced

2 cloves garlic, crushed

1 tbsp olive oil

2 red peppers, deseeded and sliced

2 yellow peppers, deseeded and sliced

2 tsp herbes de Provence

4 cod steaks or fillets

400 g (14 oz) can Heinz Cream of Tomato Soup

75 g (2¾ oz) sundried tomatoes in oil, drained and chopped

salt and freshly ground black pepper

small bunch fresh basil, torn, to serve

NOEL EDMONDS If your dinner party turns into a bit of a house party, this quick and easy recipe will save the day. Serve with a green salad or some fresh vegetables – delicious!

TUNA PASTA BAKE

1   Preheat the oven to Gas Mark 4/180°C/350°F and grease an ovenproof dish. In a bowl fold together the Macaroni Cheese, tuna and parsley then tip the mixture into the ovenproof dish.
2   Sprinkle with the breadcrumbs and the cheese and bake for 20–25 minutes, until golden and bubbling.

 Serves 2
Preparation 5 minutes
Cooking 20–25 minutes
2 x 400g (14 oz) can Heinz Macaroni Cheese
150 g (5½ oz) can tuna, drained
small bunch fresh parsley, chopped
100 g (3½ oz) fresh breadcrumbs
100 g (3½ oz) Cheddar cheese, grated

OLIVER HEATH According to Changing Rooms designer Oliver, "This dish looks good, is impressive once cooked and is very easily prepared. It tastes great served with garlic fried potatoes and steamed broccoli."

IMPRESSIVE BAKED COD

1   Preheat the oven to Gas Mark 4/180°C/350°F. Place the cod fillets in a baking tray and season.
2   Mix the other ingredients together in a small bowl and then pour over the fish. Bake for 30 minutes until bubbling and the fish is cooked through.

 Serves 2
Preparation 5 minutes
Cooking 30 minutes
2 cod or similar fish fillets
1 onion, finely chopped
1 red pepper, finely diced
4 tbsp natural yogurt
2 tbsp Heinz Garlic Sauce
salt and freshly ground black pepper

LISA FAULKNER When she's working, actress Lisa normally eats her meals in Holby City's canteen, but she's chosen a spicy Firehouse Chilli for some variety! Great for when you've finished a long shift at work and want something with a bit of a kick. Good served with rice or tortillas.

FIREHOUSE CHILLI CON CARNE

1   Heat the oil in a large frying pan or casserole and brown the mince, breaking it up with a wooden spoon. Season and remove the mince to a plate.

2   In the same pan fry the onion and garlic for 5 minutes, until softened, then replace the meat and add all the other ingredients except the fresh coriander.

3   Bring to a simmer and cook for 25 minutes, until thick. Stir in the coriander and serve with rice or tortillas, guacamole and sour cream.

Serves 4
Preparation 15 minutes
Cooking 30 minutes

1 tbsp olive oil
500g (1lb 2 oz) minced beef, lamb or pork
2 onions, peeled and sliced
2 cloves garlic, crushed
2 tsp ground cumin
2 tsp Worcestershire Sauce
1-2 small red chillis, deseeded and finely
   chopped
415 g can Heinz Baked Beans
400 g (14 oz) can Heinz Chopped Tomatoes
small bunch fresh coriander, chopped
salt and freshly ground black pepper
To serve
rice or tortillas
guacamole
sour cream

CHARLIE DIMMOCK It's no surprise that celebrity gardener Charlie Dimmock has contributed such a down-to-earth recipe. This dish can be prepared in a matter of minutes — leaving you plenty of time to get on with the gardening. Tastes even better if you grow the herbs yourself!

QUICK CASSOULET

1   Heat the oil in a large frying pan or casserole and fry the onion and garlic for 5 minutes, until softened. Add the tomatoes, herbs and celery and bring to a simmer.

2   Simmer for 10 minutes then add the remaining ingredients and simmer a further 10 minutes before serving piping hot.

Serves 4

Preparation 10 minutes

Cooking 25 minutes

1 tbsp olive oil

2 medium onions, chopped

3 cloves garlic, crushed

400 g (14 oz) can Heinz Chopped Tomatoes

2 sprigs thyme, chopped

2 sprigs marjoram, chopped

1 celery stalk, finely chopped

1 bay leaf

200 g (7 oz) thick sliced ham, cubed

2 x 415 g cans Heinz Baked Beans

small bunch parsley, chopped

salt and freshly ground black pepper

PHILIPPA FORRESTER Television presenter Philippa says "I used to bake this for an old friend of mine every time he got dumped – it's the ultimate in comfort food." A great recipe to have on standby!

POTATO AND BEAN BAKE

1   Preheat the oven to Gas Mark 5/190°C/375°F. Slice the potatoes and layer them in a 1.5 litre (2½ pint) greased ovenproof dish with the beans and half the cheese. Season and finish with a layer of potato.

2   Beat the milk, egg and herbs together then season and pour over the potatoes. Dot with the butter and sprinkle over the remaining cheese. Bake for 30 minutes and serve hot.

 Serves 4

Preparation 10 minutes
Cooking 30 minutes

1 kg (2 lb 4 oz) potatoes, par-boiled
415 g can Heinz Baked Beans
50 g (1¾ oz) Cheddar or Parmesan cheese, grated
150 ml (¼ pint) milk
1 egg
1 tsp dried tarragon or oregano
15 g (½ oz) butter
salt and freshly ground black pepper

ALICE BEER This recipe for Chicken and Vegetable Bake is Hot Property as far as television presenter Alice is concerned. Make it yourself to see just how easy it is.

EASY CHICKEN AND VEGETABLE BAKE

1   Preheat the oven to Gas Mark 4/180°C/350°F and lightly grease a large lasagne-style ovenproof dish. Place the sliced potatoes in an overlapping layer in the base of the dish.

2   In a bowl mix together the chicken, onion, vegetables, soup, parsley and seasoning then spread this mixture over the potatoes and sprinkle with the breadcrumbs and cheese.

3   Bake for 40–45 minutes, until golden and cooked through.

Serves 4

Preparation 10 minutes
Cooking 45 minutes

2 large potatoes, finely sliced
450 g (1 lb) skinless, boneless chicken thighs, diced
1 onion, peeled and finely chopped
250 g (8 oz) broccoli florets
250 g (8 oz) carrots, sliced
250 g (8 oz) peas
400 g (14 oz) can Heinz Cream of Chicken Soup
small bunch fresh parsley, chopped
100 g (3½ oz) fresh breadcrumbs
100 g (3½ oz) Cheddar Cheese, grated
salt and freshly ground black pepper

DENISE VAN OUTEN Denise, a rising theatre star and all-round entertainer, shares her favourite recipe. "This is perfect post-theatre food – it's quick and easy to make."

CHINATOWN SWEET AND SOUR PORK

1   Mix the orange with the honey and the Chinese five spice then toss the pork in this mixture. Leave to marinate for a minimum of 30 minutes, up to 8 hours.

2   In a large wok or frying pan heat the oil then stir fry the pork and its marinade for 5 minutes on a high heat. Add the onions, courgettes, nuts and sesame seeds and stir fry for a further 5–10 minutes, until golden at the edges.

3   In a bowl mix together the Ketchup, rice vinegar, soy sauce, sesame oil and cornflour to a smooth paste. Pour over the stir fry and cook for 5 more minutes, until the sauce is thick and shiny. Serve with rice or noodles.

 Serves 4

Preparation 5 minutes
+ 30 minutes to 8 hours marinating
Cooking 15 minutes

grated zest and juice of an orange

2 tbsp runny honey

2 tsp Chinese five spice powder

450 g (1 lb) pork fillet, sliced

1 tbsp olive oil

bunch spring onions, sliced into 2.5 cm (1 inch) lengths

4 large courgettes, sliced

100 g (3½ oz) cashew nuts

50 g (1¾ oz) sesame seeds

4 tbsp Heinz Tomato Ketchup

2 tbsp rice vinegar

4 tbsp soy sauce

2 tsp sesame oil

1 tbsp cornflour

rice or noodles, to serve

ALAN HANSEN This is the perfect recipe for football pundit Alan, combining the winning hat-trick of meat, vegetables and Heinz in one strike. A great way to be a winner in the kitchen!

CHICKEN AND ASPARAGUS PIE

1   Preheat the oven to Gas Mark 5/190°C/375°F and lightly grease a 1.5-litre (2¾-pint) ovenproof dish. In a bowl mix together all the ingredients except the pastry and egg, and then tip into the ovenproof dish.

2   Cut the pastry to fit the dish and use any trimmings to make shapes to go on the top. Seal with a brush of beaten egg under the edges and brush the top with the remaining egg.

3   Bake for 30 minutes, until cooked through and golden brown on top.

 Serves 4

Preparation 15 minutes
Cooking 30 minutes

4 skinless, boneless chicken breasts
small bunch fresh parsley, finely chopped
300 g (10½ oz) asparagus spears, cut into 2.5 cm (1 inch) lengths
400 g (14 oz) can Heinz Cream of Chicken Soup
150 ml (¼ pint) white wine or stock
250 g (9 oz) ready-rolled puff pastry
1 small egg, beaten

JONNY LEE MILLER According to film actor Jonny Lee Miller, "This recipe is a good mix of protein and carbohydrate. Plus the spinach is full of iron to make you strong." So it not only tastes great, it's good for you too!

CHICKEN AND SPINACH RISOTTO

1   Heat the oil in a large lidded saucepan, add the chicken and onion and cook for 5 minutes, until the chicken is browned and the onion softened.

2   Add the rice and toss to coat it in the oil. Add the soup, wine and stock and stir to mix well. Cover and bring to a simmer. Turn down the heat and simmer very gently for 25 minutes, stirring frequently, until all the liquid has been absorbed and the rice is tender and creamy.

3   Stir in the spinach and Parmesan and allow to stand for 2 minutes while the spinach wilts. Check the seasoning and serve.

 Serves 4

Preparation 10 minutes
Cooking 30 minutes

1 tbsp olive oil
1 onion, finely chopped
4 boneless, skinless chicken thighs, finely diced
200 g (7 oz) risotto rice
400 g (14 oz) can Heinz Cream of Chicken Soup
150 ml (¼ pint) white wine
300 ml (½ pint) chicken or vegetable stock
225 g (8 oz) baby spinach leaves
100 g (3½ oz) Parmesan, finely grated
salt and freshly ground black pepper

QUICK
AND EAZY
DINNERZ

66

BRIAN TURNER An Italian twist on a great British classic, from one of the country's best-loved chefs. A great recipe to satisfy even the largest of appetites.

STEAK AND PASTA PIE

1   Preheat the oven to Gas Mark 4/180°C/350°F and grease an ovenproof dish that holds approx 1.5 litres (2¾ pint).

2   Heat the oil in a large frying pan and fry the onion, garlic and mince for 5–10 minutes, until the mince is browned and the onion is softened, then season. This is best done in batches so that the mince does not stew. put half the mince into the prepared oven dish.

3   Place the Macaroni Cheese in a large bowl and add the rest of the mince, chopped tomatoes, and parsley. Fold together and spoon this mixture over the meat in the ovenproof dish. Sprinkle with the grated cheese and bake for 30 minutes, until golden brown and cooked through.

4   Serve hot or cold, allowing to cool before cutting.

 Serves 4

Preparation 20 minutes
Cooking 30 minutes

1 tbsp olive oil

1 onion, peeled and finely chopped

1 clove garlic, crushed

450 g (1 lb) minced beef

2 x 400 g (14 oz) can Heinz Macaroni Cheese

125 g (4 oz) sun-blushed or sun-dried tomatoes, chopped

small bunch fresh parsley or basil, chopped

100 g (3½ oz) Parmesan, grated

salt and freshly ground black pepper

SPECIAL MEALZ

Over the weekend it's easier to spend more time in the kitchen, and these dishes are all simple but require that little bit more effort. This chapter includes great classics to enjoy at long weekend lunches, like Hearty Beef and Beer Casserole or Roast Lemon Chicken. For entertaining with some extra style try the Moroccan Cous Cous and vegetarian specials like the delicious Spiced Courgette and Lentil Loaf.

CHAPTER

5

CILLA BLACK A great meal for lazy Sunday lunches from one of Britain's favourite stars. It smells fantastic and tastes even better – sure to be a hit with all the family.

ROAST LEMON CHICKEN WITH GARLIC

1   Preheat the oven to Gas Mark 4/180°C/350°F. Squeeze the lemon juice over the chicken then stuff the squeezed lemon quarters inside the bird's cavity. Season and scatter with the herbs then anoint with the olive oil.

2   Roast the chicken for 1 hour, until the juices run clear when it is pierced with a skewer in the flesh of the thickest part of the thigh. If the juices are pink, return it to the oven for a further 10 minutes then test again.

3 Meanwhile, make the stuffing by melting the butter in a frying pan and frying the nuts until lightly golden. Add the garlic and onion and fry for a further 3 minutes.

4   Add all the other stuffing ingredients and stir together, then spoon into a small, greased roasting tin. Add the stuffing to the oven for the last 30 minutes of the chicken's cooking time.

5   Allow the chicken to stand for 15 minutes to rest before carving and serve with spoonfuls of stuffing.

 Serves 4

Preparation 15 minutes

Cooking 1 hour

a whole chicken, about 1.5 kg (3 lb 5 oz)
1 unwaxed lemon, cut into quarters
few sprigs rosemary or thyme
1 tbsp olive oil
salt and freshly ground black pepper
For the stuffing
25 g (1 oz) butter
50 g (2 oz) chopped walnuts
1 medium onion, chopped finely
1 clove garlic, crushed
100 g (3½ oz) fresh breadcrumbs
1 egg, beaten
50 g (2 oz) dried apricots, chopped
grated zest and juice of a lemon
415 g can Heinz Baked Beans
1 cooking apple, grated

ALAN TITCHMARSH Alan Titchmarsh, one of Britain's most famous gardeners, is passionate about bringing the garden into the kitchen. "Once you've experienced the satisfying thrill of growing your own vegetables, you'll never want to settle for shop-bought veg again." Why not grow your own courgettes and try them in this great recipe?

SPICED COURGETTE AND LENTIL LOAF

1   Preheat the oven to Gas Mark 5/190°C/375°F and grease and line a 900 g (2 lb) loaf tin. Slice one of the courgettes and grate the others coarsely. Arrange the sliced courgette over the base of the tin and place all the other ingredients in a large bowl.

2   Pour the mixture into the loaf tin and bake for 1 hour. Allow to rest for 5 minutes before turning out. Serve hot or cold.

 Serves 2
Preparation 5 minutes
Cooking 1 hour

350 g (12 oz) courgettes
400 g (14 oz) can Heinz Lentil Soup
1 small onion, grated
100 g (3½ oz) fresh wholemeal breadcrumbs
100 g (3½ oz) mixed nuts, chopped
2 eggs, beaten
1 tsp ground cumin
1 tsp ground coriander
small bunch mint, chopped
salt and freshly ground black pepper

JOANNA LUMLEY One of Britain's best-loved actresses, Joanna says, "I adore Baked Beans — this is a new way of eating them." Quick and easy to prepare, we're sure you'll agree that her recipe tastes absolutely fabulous. The perfect starter to your special meal.

BEAN PÂTÉ

1   Heat the olive oil in a frying pan and gently fry the onion, garlic and cumin seeds until softened and pale golden.

2   Place this mixture in a food processor with the Tabasco, mint or chives and beans (drained of some of their sauce), and blend until smooth. Serve with the hot brown toast.

 Serves 2
Preparation + cooking 5 minutes

2 tbsp olive oil
1 large onion, finely chopped
2 cloves garlic, crushed
½ tsp cumin seeds
dash of Tabasco
small bunch fresh mint or chives, chopped
415 g can Heinz Baked Beans
salt and freshly ground black pepper
hot brown toast, to serve

SPECIAL
MEALZ

73

JENNY FROST Atomic Kitten singer Jenny offers a purrfect recipe to warm you up on cold winter nights. Serve with hot baked potatoes – it's atomic!

WINTER VEG AND BEAN GOULASH

1   Preheat the oven to Gas Mark 4/180°C/350°F. Place all the ingredients except the chives in a large casserole and stir together well.

2   Cover and bake for 1½ hours. You can bake some potatoes at the same time to serve with the goulash. Serve scattered with the chopped chives.

 Serves 4–6

Preparation 15 minutes

Cooking 1½ hours

450 g (1 lb) parsnips, cut into pieces of approx. 2.5 cm (1 inch)

450 g (1 lb) carrots, cut into pieces of approx. 2.5 cm (1 inch)

450 g (1 lb) leeks, cut into pieces of approx. 2.5 cm (1 inch)

415 g can Heinz Baked Beans

300ml (½ pint) vegetable stock or white wine

2–3 sprigs rosemary, leaves removed and finely chopped

2 tsp paprika

300 ml (½ pint) sour cream or natural yogurt

salt and freshly ground black pepper

To serve

baked potatoes

small bunch chives, chopped (optional)

BETTY DRIVER This recipe gives away all the secrets of Coronation Street's famous hot pot. Says Betty, "It's great! I like to serve it with pickled cabbage, beetroot or chutney."

LANCASHIRE HOTPOT

1   Preheat the oven to Gas Mark 4/180°C/350°F and grease a large casserole or oven-proof dish with the olive oil. Place a layer of potatoes on the bottom and arrange the cutlets on top.

2   Sprinkle in the onions, carrots, herbs and sugar and season well. Pour over the soup and stock and finish with a layer of potatoes arranged so that the slices overlap one another.

3   Cover and bake for 2 hours, removing the cover for the last 30 minutes so that the potatoes turn golden and crispy.

 Serves 4

Preparation 15 minutes

Cooking 2 hours

1 tbsp olive oil

800 g (1 lb 11 oz) potatoes, sliced thinly

600 g (1 lb 5 oz) lamb cutlets

3 medium onions, chopped finely

2 medium carrots, sliced thinly

4 sprigs thyme, chopped

1 bay leaf

a pinch of sugar

400 g (14 oz) can Heinz Spring Vegetable Soup

300 ml (½ pint) vegetable stock

25 g (1 oz) butter, melted

salt and freshly ground black pepper

JOHN CLEESE Comic legend John Cleese says "I was astonished to discover the delights of North African cuisine while I was in Tunisia shooting *Life of Brian*. Moroccan Lamb Cous-Cous is almost indistinguishable from Tunisian Lamb Cous Cous. It is recommended that before starting to eat, all the diners shout 'I'm Brian!' three times very loudly."

MOROCCAN LAMB COUS COUS

1   Preheat the oven to Gas Mark 3/170°C/320°C. Heat half the oil in a large casserole and brown the lamb, then use a slotted spoon to remove it to a plate.

2   Heat the other half of the oil in the same pan and fry the onion and garlic for 5 minutes, until softened. Add the other vegetables and replace the lamb.

3   Add all the other ingredients except the coriander, bring to the boil, then cover and bake in the oven for 1 hour. Check the seasoning and serve scattered with the coriander on a bed of cous cous.

 Serves 6

Preparation 15 minutes

Cooking 1 hour 15 minutes

600 g (1 lb 5 oz) lamb, cut into bite-sized
    pieces, or Quorn pieces

4 tbsp olive oil

2 onions, chopped

2 cloves garlic, crushed

1 large courgette, diced

1 medium aubergine, diced

1 red pepper, de-seeded and diced

1 tbsp ground cumin or cumin seeds

1 tsp dried chilli flakes

2 tsp ground tumeric

1 cinnamon stick

2 x 200 g (7 oz) can Heinz Curried Baked Beans

3 tbsp Heinz Sundried Tomato Sauce or Tomato
    Ketchup

400 g (14 oz) can chickpeas

600 ml (1 pint) vegetable stock

salt and freshly ground black pepper

small bunch fresh coriander, chopped, to serve

KEREN WOODHEAD & SARA DALLIN It ain't what you do with this dish from girl band Bananarama, it's the way that you do it ... This is traditional British cooking at its best – great for all the family.

HEARTY BEEF AND BEER CASSEROLE

1   Cut the meat into 3 cm (1¼ inch) pieces and toss in the seasoned flour. Heat the oil in a large casserole and brown the meat on all sides.

2   Add the beer and simmer, uncovered, for 5 minutes. Add the onion, carrot, celery, parsnip and soup and bring back to a simmer. Cover and cook gently for 1 hour, until tender and thick.

Serves 4–6
Preparation 15 minutes
Cooking 1 hour

500 g (1 lb 5 oz) stewing steak
50 g (1¾ oz) seasoned plain flour
2 tbsp olive oil
355 ml (12 fl oz) can dark beer or Guinness
1 large onion, roughly chopped
2 large carrots, roughly chopped
2 stalks celery, trimmed and chopped
2 large parsnips, roughly chopped
400 g (14 oz) can Heinz Giant Minestrone Soup

MICHAEL BUERK Newsreader Michael Buerk is a keen supporter of I CAN. "Communicating is what I do. But expressing thoughts and feelings, and understanding those of others, is something 1 in 10 children struggle with. That is why I CAN's work is so vital. Every child deserves to fulfill their potential, because living in silence isn't always golden."

LAMB AND APRICOT STEW

1   Drain and chop the apricots, reserving the juice. Put the lamb, spices, onion, apricot juice and just enough water to cover in a heavy-bottomed pan or casserole and bring to the boil. Cover and simmer gently for 1½ hours until there is a rich sauce.

2   Add the apricots, beans and honey and heat through then check the seasoning and serve sprinkled with the fresh mint.

Serves 4
Preparation 10 minutes
Cooking 2 hours

400 g (14 oz) can apricots in juice
400 g (14 oz) lamb steaks, cubed
¼ tsp ground ginger
½ tsp ground coriander
1 tsp ground cinnamon
1 medium onion, chopped finely
415 g can Heinz Baked Beans
1 tbsp runny honey
salt and freshly ground black pepper
small bunch fresh mint, chopped, to serve

SPECIAL
MEALZ

INDEX